DEAD RECKONING

DEAD RECKONING

by Eric Chappell

JOSEF WEINBERGER PLAYS

LONDON

DEAD RECKONING
First published in 2012
by Josef Weinberger Ltd
12-14 Mortimer Street, London W1T 3JJ
www.josef-weinberger.com / plays@jwmail.co.uk

ISBN: 978 0 85676 337 3

Printed by Commercial Colour Press plc, Hainault, Essex

CAST OF CHARACTERS

Megan – *late 30s*

Todd – *40s*

Tony – *40s*

Slater – *late 30s*

The action takes place in Anthony Reed's study overlooking a London park. The time is the present.

Dead Reckoning was first presented by Outloud Productions on 23rd September 2010 at the Dixon Studio, Palace Theatre, Westcliff-on-Sea with the following cast.

Todd...................................George Kemp

Tony Reed.......................... Rocky Rising

Megan Reed .... Sally Lawrence

Slater ....John Frost

Directed by Kate Beales

Lighting by Rachel Stoneley

Set Design by Graham Hull

ACT ONE

ANTHONY REED'S *study. Early evening. Large sash windows overlook a park. The room is elegantly furnished. A door stage right leads to the hall.*

A door stage left leads to a store room.

A large table lamp, already lit, emphasises the gathering gloom. A few books are scattered around. There is an air of casual good taste.

TODD *is gazing out of the windows. He is a man in his forties. He is greying slightly and wears glasses. He is wearing a plain raincoat. He turns as* MEGAN REED *enters the room. She is late thirties, attractive in a faded way with shadows under her eyes. She is holding* TODD'S *card in her hand which she waves and places on the desk.*

MEGAN	I've told him you're waiting but I'm not sure he'll see you.
TODD	I thought he was considering it?
MEGAN	He is but only to be rude I'm afraid.
TODD	Rude?
	(MEGAN *taps the card on the desk.*)
MEGAN	Penal Reform. He hates everything that smacks of reform. My husband's close to the Taliban in these matters. If you knew his views –
TODD	But I do, Mrs Reed. I've read about them. That's why he'd be such a catch.

MEGAN   I admire your optimism, Mr Todd but I'm
             afraid you're wasting your time. In fact, I can't
             really understand why you came.

TODD   Oh, perhaps we're not so very far apart – and I
             can be quite persuasive.

MEGAN   Mr Todd, you couldn't be further apart – and he
             is very busy . . .

TODD   I hope I'm not interrupting the creative flow?

MEGAN   He has an exhibition very soon.

TODD   Oh dear. I'd hate to come between him and his
             work.

MEGAN   No one does that, Mr Todd.

TODD   And so they shouldn't. After all, art is long, life
             is short. No one knows that better than your
             husband . . .

             (*He sighs and looks over the park. She regards
             him thoughtfully.*)

MEGAN   Do you admire his work?

TODD   I have a small Anthony Reed I'm rather proud
             of. One from his early years, when they weren't
             quite so expensive. One of the bright, happy
             ones, before he entered his sombre period.
             (*Another sigh.*) All perfectly understandable of
             course . . .

             (*She studies him again, a thing she continues
             to do during their conversation. He catches her
             glance. He returns it.*)

             You know, I do believe you are in my picture.

MEGAN   I was his model once.

TODD   But not anymore?

MEGAN   No.

TODD   I thought I recognised you.

MEGAN   You surprise me. I've changed a great deal.

TODD   And now he has another model.

MEGAN   Yes.

TODD   She appears quite often.

MEGAN   Yes. But then she doesn't change . . .

            (*Silence.*)

            (TODD *looks around the room.*)

TODD   One thing surprises me – there are no pictures.

MEGAN   No. (*Smiles.*) I'll let you into a little secret – he
            doesn't care for pictures.

TODD   Even his own?

MEGAN   Particularly his own.

TODD   I can understand that.

MEGAN   (*sharply*) Why?

TODD   I suppose he likes to get away from his work –
            one needs a break – one needs to relax. And his
            pictures are disturbing to say the least. Do they
            disturb Mr Reed?

MEGAN   I've no idea. They don't seem to disturb the
             public.

TODD   No but then people like to be frightened, at least
             by a painting . . . How things change. A few
             years ago he was virtually selling his pictures
             off the railings – then he was taken up and he's
             never looked back. Nothing but success. The
             darker he becomes the more successful. How
             things turn out; after a tragedy that would have
             finished most men; fame and fortune. Life does
             have a way of compensating . . .

MEGAN   Mr Todd, you are here about penal reform? You
             sound like a fan.

TODD   I am. And I want to ask him something.

MEGAN   What?

TODD   Why his pictures have such cheerful subjects
             in the foreground – children playing,
             lovers meeting, ladies strolling – and in the
             background – those shadows creeping nearer
             – those shadows and that figure. It is a figure?
             I'm never quite sure.

MEGAN   But you think it maybe?

TODD   It seems to be growing more substantial but
             then so do the shadows. One day, I swear, his
             pictures will be all shadows.

MEGAN   Mr Todd, I wouldn't ask him. He doesn't
             discuss his pictures.

TODD   Pity.

MEGAN   You seem to have made a study of him.

TODD	I'd like to know him better – and what better way than through his pictures? 'By my works ye shall know me'.
MEGAN	Why should you wish to know him better?
TODD	So that I can help him.
MEGAN	I thought the idea was for him to help you?
TODD	In a strange way I feel our needs are mutual.
MEGAN	I don't think so. (*Pause.*) There's something unsaid in this conversation, isn't there?
TODD	Is there?
MEGAN	Something we're skirting around.
TODD	You're very perceptive.
MEGAN	Don't flatter me. You're here because of what happened to my husband, aren't you?
TODD	Ah, we've reached it.
MEGAN	What?
TODD	The unsaid.
MEGAN	Yes – and I'd prefer it to remain unsaid. I've lived with the unsaid for many years. I'd like to keep it that way.
TODD	But your husband hasn't left it unsaid, Mrs Reed.
MEGAN	Perhaps not in public but it remains unsaid here. And I don't think it'll help your cause to mention it.

TODD   Is he so unpredictable on the subject?

MEGAN   No – he's predictable. Only too predictable.
            What happened has given him a distorted view
            of things . . .

TODD   You mean . . . unbalanced?

MEGAN   I mean distorted. Which reveals itself in
            displays of bad temper and tasteless jokes. I
            advise you not to talk about the shadows in his
            pictures – and I wouldn't talk about the past at
            all.

TODD   You feel he lacks a certain resilience where the
            unsaid is concerned?

MEGAN   I'm not worried about his resilience – I'm
            worried about yours.

TODD   You make him sound quite formidable.

MEGAN   He can be.

TODD   I'm not confrontational, Mrs Reed. Never have
            been. I like to creep up on a subject as it were.
            Perhaps my visit was a mistake. Would you
            prefer me to leave?

MEGAN   Too late. He knows you're here. He'll think I
            sent you away.

TODD   I hope you don't mind me saying this but you
            sound afraid of him.

MEGAN   I'm afraid of his moods.

TODD   Is that why you're no longer his model? After
            all, you're still a beautiful woman.

MEGAN   You're flattering me again, Mr Todd. I'm no
           longer his model because he found a better one.

TODD   Who is she?

MEGAN   Mr Todd, I think you keep asking me questions
           to which you know the answer. The model he
           uses now is Alison – his first wife.

TODD   But she's dead.

MEGAN   Dead but not forgotten. And she won't grow old
           as we shall grow old, Mr Todd.

TODD   That's very strange. Is he obsessed with her
           memory?

MEGAN   We still live here. We still overlook the park.
           He habitually includes her in his pictures. What
           do you think?

TODD   I suppose that explains his well publicised
           desire for revenge.

MEGAN   It's not healthy, is it?

TODD   Revenge? I don't know if it's healthy – it
           certainly isn't legal – but it is understandable.

MEGAN   Is it? You should have come here on the
           anniversary of her death. There'd have been a
           large picture of Alison in the drawing room and
           candles burning on either side. All her friends
           would have been here, remembering her – her
           kindness, her sayings, her sweet gestures –
           whilst I served the drinks.

TODD   You don't agree with this excessive mourning?

MEGAN   It's his way of dealing with it I suppose.

TODD   But it's hard on you.

MEGAN   It's not easy to follow a saint, Mr Todd.

TODD   I suppose not. But as you say, it's his way of dealing with it. As is, I suppose, his bloodthirsty sense of justice.

MEGAN   That's not justice, that's vengeance.

TODD   Again, perfectly natural.

MEGAN   Natural?

TODD   Don't underestimate the strength of our natural instincts, Mrs Reed. Most modern symptoms of madness are only the call of the wild – a return to our primitive past.

MEGAN   But you agree it's madness?

TODD   Oh, yes.

MEGAN   Then what's the point in talking to him?

TODD   Research, mainly. The law has punished but Mr Reed feels the law has failed him. I want to help him come to terms with that.

MEGAN   You'll never do it.

TODD   We know the system isn't perfect. Because of this we feel it's as important to consult the victims of crime as it is to consider the perpetrators. See what we can amend.

MEGAN   Amend?

TODD   Reform, Mrs Reed.

MEGAN   Mr Todd, I'm beginning to recognise a quality
          in you that worries me.

TODD   What's that, Mrs Reed?

MEGAN   Persistence.

TODD   I do have a gentle persistence – people have
          remarked on it.

MEGAN   Some might call it interference. And when you
          interfere in people's lives – things can happen.

TODD   You're alarming me again.

MEGAN   You're the sort of person he hates most. High
          on the list and it's a long list. Reformers –
          do-gooders – bleeding hearts. Don't take it
          personally – as I said – it's a *long* list.

TODD   And are you on that list, Mrs Reed?

MEGAN   (*stares*) What made you say that?

TODD   The way you said it. Sorry I spoke – I'm sure
          I'm wrong.

MEGAN   Not entirely.

TODD   But why should he hate you?

MEGAN   Can't you guess?

TODD   Tell me.

MEGAN   Because I'm alive.

TODD   And she isn't?

MEGAN   After it happened he hated everyone – everyone
               who lived. Disasters, earthquakes, train
               wrecks left him unmoved. He gloated over the
               casualties, the death of strangers – even the
               death of friends. Above all he hated the people
               who kept her murderer alive – people like you,
               Mr Todd.

TODD   I can understand him hating me, Mrs Reed, but
               you? Why did he marry you if he felt that way?

MEGAN   (*smiles*) He couldn't sleep – he had nightmares
               – and I was at hand.

TODD   At hand? Is that all? Did he have no feelings
               for you?

MEGAN   He had once.

TODD   But not now?

MEGAN   He's not rational on the subject of Alison.

TODD   That's where I think I can help. They say he
               who studies revenge keeps his wound green. I
               can heal that wound. He's living a nightmare,
               Mrs Reed.

MEGAN   He's not living a nightmare, Mr Todd – I am.
               (*Pause.*) There's another reason why he may
               hate me.

TODD   What's that?

MEGAN   On the night she died we were here, together . . .

TODD   Ah.

MEGAN   She wanted him to go with her. There'd been a
               mugging in the park. But he chose to stay here

with me – he said it was to finish a picture. He
said she'd be safe with the dog – it was a big
dog.

TODD   But the dog ran away.

MEGAN   How did you know that?

TODD   I read the reports.

MEGAN   Now I walk a dog in the park – and it's quite
a small dog. But it doesn't seem to worry him.
Apparently there's only room for so much
anguish.

TODD   Why are you telling me this?

MEGAN   Because when he begins his lamentations you'll
see another side. It gives his grief another
dimension.

TODD   I'm sorry. I didn't know.

MEGAN   At last I've told you something you didn't
know.

TODD   I didn't know but I'm not surprised. Aren't
artists supposed to fall in love with their
models?

MEGAN   No – models fall in love with the artist,
unfortunately. They see themselves formed and
shaped by him everyday. He becomes a god to
them.

TODD   Is that how you felt?

MEGAN   Yes.

TODD   But he didn't – feel the same way about you?

MEGAN   He did for a time. But then he fell in love with
           Alison.

TODD   Once she was dead?

MEGAN   So much more convenient. At least you don't
           quarrel.

TODD   And he's never ceased to blame himself.

MEGAN   He's never ceased to blame me.

TODD   And everyone else it seems. I can see it now.
           He's suppressing his guilt in this implacable
           hatred of her murderer.

MEGAN   He always said he could kill Sweeney with his
           bare hands.

TODD   Sweeney?

MEGAN   The man who killed her.

TODD   He doesn't mean that?

MEGAN   I think he does. So you see talking to him
           would be rather a waste of time.

TODD   Then why did you give him my card?

MEGAN   He knows when we have visitors. He doesn't
           like to be ignored. But since I've told him you
           were here – and since he hasn't come down. I'll
           say you grew tired of waiting.

TODD   But I haven't, Mrs Reed. And since he feels
           everyone's failed him how can I do the same?

MEGAN   But Tony's intractable where reform's
           concerned.

TODD   Even so . . . if I could talk to him. You've been
            very frank with me, Mrs Reed. But have you
            told me everything?

MEGAN   What else is there to tell?

TODD   Possibly the unsaid . . . ?

MEGAN   (*hesitates*) There is one other thing – he's
            drinking heavily.

TODD   That does make reasoning difficult.

MEGAN   Perhaps another day . . .

            (*She is guiding* TODD *towards the door when*
            TONY REED *enters. They stand uncertainly.*
            TONY *is about forty. He is bearded, unkempt
            with a wild mane of hair. His eyes are red
            and sunken. He is wearing a rumpled, open
            necked shirt and has a canvas under his arm.
            He crosses to the store room door without a
            word. He opens the door and almost throws the
            canvas inside. He turns back to the desk and
            pours himself a glass of wine.*)

MEGAN   Do you want me to look at it?

TONY   No.

MEGAN   As bad as that?

TONY   I've done worse.

            (*He picks up the visiting card and studies* TODD.)

            Leaving already?

MEGAN   This is Mr Todd.

TONY   I know who he is. Have a drink.

TODD   I don't drink.

TONY   Why doesn't that surprise me?

            (*He studies the level in the bottle.*)

            Get me another.

            (MEGAN *stares at him coldly.*)

MEGAN   Let me take your coat, Mr Todd.

            (*She takes* TODD's *coat. She gives* TONY *an icy
            stare and exits.*)

TONY   (*smiles*) She won't of course. She doesn't
            approve. Are you married, Mr Todd?

TODD   No.

TONY   Lucky you. It's a prison without bars – and
            there's no remission, even for good behaviour,
            not that there's been much of that.

TODD   I'm sure it has its compensations, Mr Reed.

TONY   I can't think of any at the moment.

TODD   Your wife's an attractive woman . . .

TONY   Window dressing, Mr Todd. There's a belief
            that women go off sex as they grow older – it's
            not true. They merely go off their husbands.
            (*Regards* TODD.) Have I shocked you?

TODD   (*smiles*) I don't shock easily.

TONY   (*holds up card*) Reform?

TODD   Yes.

TONY   Why come to me?

TODD   We feel we should listen to the victims of crime.

TONY   Too true. Are you with the government?

TODD   No, we're a small, independent organisation.

TONY   I'm not giving you any money.

TODD   I'm interested in your views.

TONY   They're well known.

TODD   But that was some time ago. Said in the heat of the moment.

TONY   I haven't cooled, Mr Todd.

TODD   But since the man's paid his debt to society . . .

TONY   He may have paid his debt to society – he hasn't paid his debt to me.

TODD   How can he do that?

TONY   They say only death cancels all debts . . .

TODD   Would you really bring back hanging?

TONY   With one slight amendment.

TODD   Oh, what's that?

TONY   I'd like it to take place in public.

TODD   Surely not.

TONY   It was very popular in the old days. People
            would go miles for a hanging. You couldn't get
            near Tyburn for the crowds. Which proves one
            thing.

TODD   What's that?

TONY   Give the public what they want and they'll turn
            out.

TODD   But do they want it?

TONY   They've always wanted it.

            (*He crosses to the window and looks out.*)

            Hang someone from a tree out there and there'd
            be thousands to see it.

TODD   No.

TONY   The caterers would make a fortune. (*He turns.*)
            'The clock strikes twelve – it's dark midnight.
            Yet the Magpie and Stump is a blaze of light.
            The parties are met – the tables are set.
            And there is M'fuse. And Lieutenant Tregooze.
            And there is Sir Carnaby Jenks of the Blues.
            All come to see a man die in his shoes.'
            Ingoldsby . . .

TODD   That was pseudonym. The author was Barham.
            And it was written in a tone of mockery about
            something he saw as barbaric.

TONY   (*sharply*) Barbaric! There's a word that's
            over-used. It's lost its meaning, Mr Todd. They
            say that fox hunting's barbaric. They say that
            punishing your children is barbaric. They'll

soon be saying that smoking in public places is barbaric – that dogs fouling the footpath is barbaric. What word will they then reserve for murder? For the first time in the civilised world convicted murderers can walk the streets – that is barbaric, Mr Todd.

TODD Men can change.

TONY Men like that don't change.

TODD You talk very lightly of hanging but suppose the man is innocent? That could happen. It has happened.

TONY Then I hope I'd have the strength of character to live with it.

TODD Surely he'd need the strength of character. He has to *die* with it.

TONY Mr Todd, we inject children against disease – sometimes a child dies but we still keep injecting – for the greater good.

TODD You see the death penalty in that light – for the greater good?

TONY (*shrugs*) It's not perfect but it's the only way. We sentence a man to seven years for burglary, later we find he's innocent. We can't give him back those seven years – and we still keep sentencing.

TODD The death penalty is a little more final. We could be guilty of taking an innocent life.

TONY Not guilty. Guilt comes from intent. If there's no intent to take an innocent life, there's no guilt. It's an act of God.

TODD   You blame God?

TONY   I think you'll find he even sanctions it.

TODD   Have you ever considered that your attitude
        may have become hardened by experience?

TONY   Yes.

TODD   Then you'd kill for revenge.

TONY   There's nothing wrong with revenge. It's
        a better motive than to kill for twenty-five
        pounds, one credit card and some jewellery.

TODD   Is that what he took?

TONY   That was what her life was worth to him.

TODD   (*sympathetically*) She's at peace now, Mr Reed.

TONY   How do you know? If I were to cut your throat
        right now how would you feel – apart from a
        sudden loss of appetite? You'd feel, why me?
        You'd cry for justice – for punishment.

TODD   But he has been punished.

TONY   You call that punishment? Do you know what
        they used to do? Drag them on a hurdle to
        Tyburn – hang them – cut them down while
        still alive – castrate them – slit their stomachs
        open – pull out their intestines and burn them
        before their dying eyes – then cut them into
        pieces and leave the parts around the city as
        a warning – they'd even pickle their heads so
        you'd recognise the bastards years later. Those
        were the days, Mr Todd. And I'd have gloried
        in it.

(TODD *looks at him in silence for a moment.
clears his throat.*)

TODD   That would be a subjective reaction.

TONY   Of course I'm being subjective. Is there any
other way? I lost my wife at the hands of a
drunken drifter. And don't say he may have
been innocent. They found his footprints near
her body. There was blood on his hands. He had
her possessions. He had a record. And I saw
him from that very window hurrying from the
park at the time of the murder.

TODD   But suppose the footprints weren't near
the body – suppose the body was near the
footprints? Footprints made earlier. Suppose
he'd found your wife's possessions and kept
them to finance his drinking. Suppose he was
innocent?

TONY   As I've told you already – that's a risk I'd be
prepared to take.

TODD   Personally?

TONY   Any time. I'd be prepared to pull the lever,
throw the switch, press the button.

TODD   Surely not.

TONY   Try me. I'd not only do it, I'd have a good
night's sleep afterwards and eat a hearty
breakfast.

TODD   I believe you would. But even if he was guilty
– he was a sick man – his reason destroyed by
drink.

TONY   My God! You're all the same. You're making
            excuses for him. You're going to tell me his
            parents didn't love him. That he had trouble
            with his potty during infancy. He's not to blame
            – all he needs is rehabilitation, a roomier cell,
            a larger tv, a well equipped gym, and a course
            in pottery. Is that a punishment? Did you know
            it costs as much to keep a murderer in prison
            as it does to keep a boy at Eton – and with the
            same disastrous results. They both gain a false
            sense of privilege. And why do they do it?
            Because the lawyers need criminals – just as
            the criminals need lawyers. They feed off each
            other. The lawyers don't want them in prison
            – they certainly don't want them dead. There's
            no money in that. They want them alive and
            on the streets, so they can transgress further
            and make them more money – more money for
            those ambulance chasers, trimmers and fine
            tuners, with a dozen technicalities up their
            sleeves. And do you know why we put up with
            it? Because virtue has lost its nerve.

TODD   That's quite a speech.

TONY   There's plenty more where that came from.
            Well, I may not be able to kill him but I hope
            he rots in that prison.

TODD   But he's not rotting, Mr Reed.

TONY   (*stares*) What?

TODD   He's out.

TONY   But he hasn't served his full term.

TODD   Nevertheless, he's been released on license.

TONY	My God! Has he fooled them? Don't say he's a changed man. Don't tell me he's found God. I couldn't bear that.
TODD	I don't know but he was a model prisoner.
TONY	(*frowns*) Even so – they wouldn't have let him out unless . . .
TODD	Unless he'd come to terms with what he'd done and accepted his guilt . . .
TONY	Then he's confessed.
TODD	It would appear so.
TONY	After all these years of maintaining his innocence he confesses! His lawyer will be disappointed – I think he was planning another lucrative appeal. Still, there will be more work for him now our friend is out.
TODD	But suppose he has learned his lesson and become a decent member of society. How would you feel if you were to meet him?
TONY	I'd kill him.
TODD	Surely not. You'd go to prison. Is he worth it?
TONY	Oh, yes. I'll tell you a little story. There was once a Corsican peasant who discovered his wife in adultery and killed her. He spent thirty years in prison. He served his sentence quietly and without complaint. The day he was released he returned to his village and killed his wife's lover. He returned to prison, quite contented, to serve out the rest of his days. He'd been avenged.

TODD   And you'd do the same?

TONY   Yes. So you see you're wasting your time. I'm quite unreformable.

TODD   But you don't know what my reforms are. (*He leans forward. Long pause.*) I want to bring it back . . .

                (*He looks almost gleeful.*)

TONY   (*stares*) Bring what back?

TODD   The death penalty, in certain cases.

TONY   But I thought . . .

TODD   I know.

TONY   (*laughs uneasily*) Then you have my vote. (*Pause.*) What certain cases?

TODD   (*pause*) In the certain case of . . . Sweeney.

TONY   (*stares*) But he's served his time.

TODD   I know. But as you say that's hardly a punishment.

TONY   But you can't take a man after years of imprisonment and execute him.

TODD   Why not? They do it in America all the time.

TONY   What are we talking about? It could never happen here.

TODD   But it can. It can happen tonight.

TONY   What do you mean?

TODD   I came here with a proposition – but I had to be
              sure of you before I made it. I'll kill Sweeney
              for ten thousand pounds.

              (TONY *stares at him uncomprehendingly.*)

TONY   What?

TODD   Why don't you have another drink, Mr Reed. I
              think there's some left in the bottle . . .

              (*He pours* TONY *another drink.*)

TONY   You're joking of course. I suppose this is
              another way of getting your point across.

TODD   I've never been more serious. I've done
              it before. Would you like to see my press
              cuttings?

              (*He reaches in his pocket.*)

TONY   No! You're mad.

TODD   Be fair, Mr Reed – did I accuse you of madness
              when you talked of killing Sweeney?

              (TONY *picks up the card and studies.*)

TONY   Your society does this?

TODD   (*smiles*) There's no society – only me. Anyone
              can have a card printed.

TONY   And you're paid to do it?

TODD   Yes. By the victim's relatives. People who,
              like yourself, feel the law has failed them. And
              when the law has failed man – man must amend
              the law. They're quite happy to pay.

TONY   They pay you ten thousand pounds?

TODD   Perhaps you don't think your loved one is
        worth ten thousand pounds?

TONY   I didn't say that.

TODD   She's certainly worth more than twenty-five
        pounds and some pieces of jewellery. Don't you
        agree?

TONY   Yes.

TODD   Look at it as a magnificent memorial to her –
        that would cost you almost as much. Well? You
        said try me. I'm trying you. Are you going to
        be found wanting?

TONY   But you misled me.

TODD   Or have you misled me? Has this all been
        posturing? All words and gestures? The empty
        fury of a wine drinker? You have the anger and
        the hate but do you have the spirit for revenge?
        Perhaps you never loved your wife.

TONY   I did.

TODD   You let her go out into the night alone. You
        knew the dangers.

TONY   She had the dog.

TODD   The dog ran away.

TONY   He was a fierce dog.

TODD   The mystery of the dog that didn't bite. Rather
        like you, Tony, when it comes down to it.
        You bark but you don't bite. If you loved her

why did you let her walk in the park alone whilst you stayed here and made love to your mistress?

(TONY *looks at him appalled.*)

TONY   She told you that?

TODD   She didn't have to. After all, you did marry with indecent haste. Perhaps you protest too much.

TONY   What do you mean?

TODD   Perhaps Sweeney did you a favour.

(TONY *leaps up angrily.*)

TONY   Don't you dare say that! All right. Kill him.

TODD   I will. But first let me explain what will happen to Sweeney. I shall kill him but I'll need an accomplice.

TONY   An accomplice? Why?

TODD   To help me dispose of him. And the only person I can trust is you. You have what they call a vested interest.

TONY   Look, I've no intention of being caught.

TODD   (*smiles*) Not much of the Corsican peasant about you, Tony. But don't worry, you won't be caught. You don't have to do anything, only help me afterwards . . .

TONY   (*pause*) Do you know where to find him?

TODD   I have found him. I traced him to a hostel
            where he's living under an assumed name.
            Joe Sweeney has now become Joe Slater – he
            clearly wishes to bury his past – and with a past
            like his you can hardly blame him. Of course I
            wasn't as tactless as to mention his past.

TONY   You've spoken to him?

TODD   I've won his trust. And I can assure you he
            hasn't found God. He's drifting back into his
            old wicked ways . . .

TONY   (*pauses*) Where would you do it?

TODD   Here.

TONY   What!

TODD   Can you think of a better place? He has no
            friends here. No hostile witnesses. (*Smiles.*) It
            will also give you that long deferred pleasure
            of seeing a man die in his shoes . . . Unless
            your interest was purely . . . literary . . .

            (TONY *recognises the contempt in his voice.*)

TONY   It wasn't but there's my wife to consider.

TODD   Doesn't she walk the dog?

TONY   She will be doing – before it's too dark – whilst
            there are people about.

TODD   So she'll be going soon?

TONY   Yes.

TODD   How long will that take?

TONY   Only half an hour.

TODD   Time enough.

TONY   Look, I don't mind you killing him, but not here.

TODD   Tony, if you don't see it done – how do you
know it's been done? No – this is the best way

TONY   But he'll recognise me.

TODD   No, you've changed, Tony. The years haven't
been kind, in fact, to be frank, you look like
shit. Whereas prison has suited our friend –
clean living I suppose. He's no longer dull eyed
and unshaven. No women, no alcohol, work-
outs in the gym. He's a fine figure of a man.
I can assure you, you'd pass each other in the
street without knowing.

TONY   (*grimly*) I'd know him.

TODD   Perhaps you would. The one who receives
the wound has a better memory of it than the
one who inflicts it. Should I fetch him – he's
waiting in the car.

TONY   He's waiting?

TODD   Yes.

TONY   I'm not sure that I can watch it happen.

TODD   Tony, you were prepared to do it yourself a
moment ago. Now you're not sure. Think of
Alison – think of her unquiet spirit. You failed
her once – are you going to fail her again?

TONY   Will you let me think!

TODD   Should I tell you why he's here? There's an
              irony in this. He's here to kill you.

TONY   Kill me?

TODD   Possibly. As I said he's drifting back into his
              old wicked ways. I told him you owed me
              money – ten thousand pounds. That's all he
              knows about you. He's here to make sure you
              pay – if you don't he's going to kill you. Don't
              worry, it won't come to that.

TONY   But he's a murderer – he's dangerous.

TODD   He's been drinking. We'll make sure he
              continues to drink. It shouldn't be too difficult.

TONY   But it's too early for this – suppose someone
              calls?

TODD   (*frowns*) The time doesn't suit me either but Joe
              has a date. He's keen – he's sent her flowers.
              And he doesn't want to keep the lady waiting.
              But I'm afraid she'll be waiting a long time –
              the carnations will be long since wilted before
              they meet again.

              (TONY *crosses to the window.*)

TONY   But the neighbours – they're still coming home.

TODD   I know. We'll have to dispose of the body when
              it's quiet.

              (*He looks around the room.*)

              Where does that door lead?

TONY   Nowhere, it's a store room.

TODD	Does it lock?
TONY	Yes – the key's in the door.
TODD	What's it used for?
TONY	Paints, old canvases. Rubbish mainly.
TODD	Rubbish? Then it would be perfect for Joe. The next step is to get your wife out of the house.
TONY	(*pause*) What will happen afterwards?
TODD	How will we dispose of him?
TONY	Yes.
TODD	I usually burn them.
TONY	What!
TODD	That way there are no suspicious marks.
TONY	Marks?
TODD	From this.

(*He takes a noose from his pocket.*)

It's a garrotte.

TONY	A garrotte! My God!
TODD	You're beginning to disappoint me again, Tony. I thought we'd agreed on this.
TONY	We have but –

TODD   I think once you've met him you'll forget your
              qualms. You'll know what we're doing is right.
              But I don't want to rush you. I know all this is
              rather sudden. Tell you what I'll do. I'll bring
              Joe in. If you're overcome by his natural charm
              and vivacity and wish to spare him – ask for
              twenty four hours in which to pay. I'll take that
              as a sign. I'll pretend to accept your offer and
              we'll leave – no harm done. But if you make
              out the cheque – then I'll know we're off to the
              races. Signing that cheque will be like signing
              his death warrant – isn't that what you've
              always wanted to do?

TONY   But he'll be suspicious. He'll recognise the
              park – it's the scene of his crime.

TODD   One park's very much like another. And I
              brought him the back way. He doesn't know
              where he is.

TONY   But –

TODD   Tony, don't put anymore obstacles in our way
              – murder's difficult enough. But then, it's
              not murder really, is it? It's just a question of
              numbers. When nations kill, it's war. When
              society kills, it's justice. When one man kills,
              it's murder.

              (MEGAN *enters.* TODD *slips the garrotte into
              his pocket.* MEGAN *is carrying a bottle of wine
              which she places on the desk in silence.* TONY
              looks surprised at this second bottle.)

MEGAN   I'll walk the dog now – it's growing dark.

TODD   Aren't you afraid – after all that's happened?

MEGAN   No.

TODD   I would be. But then I've always been nervous
            of the dark. You never know what's lurking
            in the shadows . . . (*Turns.*) I'll be back in a
            moment, Tony.

            (*He exits.* MEGAN *stares after him.*)

MEGAN   Tony? He's grown very chummy.

TONY   Yes.

MEGAN   I'm surprised it went so well.

TONY   What?

MEGAN   Your meeting.

TONY   We have more in common that you think.

            (*She watches him pour the wine.*)

MEGAN   What's the matter? Under that alcoholic flush
            you look quite pale – as if you've seen a ghost.

TONY   Not yet – but I'm going to.

MEGAN   What do you mean?

TONY   He's brought Sweeney here.

MEGAN   (*alarmed*) Sweeney! You mean he's out? He
            can't be. He hasn't served his time.

TONY   I know. After all these years of protesting his
            innocence he finally confessed. He's out on
            license. He promised to be a good little boy and
            they sent him out with a pat on the head.

MEGAN   And Todd brought him here. Why for God's
            sake?

TONY   (*hesitates*) He wants me to meet him.

MEGAN   But now he knows where we live.

TONY   He could have found that out easily enough.

MEGAN   Haven't you suffered enough? What does Todd
            want you to do – forgive him?

TONY   No, strangely enough, he doesn't.

MEGAN   Are you sure? Isn't that the modern trend? For
            the murderer to meet the victim's family for
            cosy get togethers and forgiveness? You're not
            falling for that, surely? You said you'd never
            forgive him. You said he'd have to be dead
            first.

TONY   I know what I said, Megan.

MEGAN   He'll want something.

TONY   (*stares*) You're shaking.

MEGAN   I haven't had as much wine as you've had. It's
            clouding your judgement. You shouldn't meet
            him. You should call the police. He'll harass
            you. He'll want money.

TONY   Why should I give him money?

MEGAN   He'll want you to pay him for all those years in
            prison.

TONY   What has that to do with me?

MEGAN   You identified him.

TONY   The evidence was overwhelming. He can't
            blame me.

MEGAN   His mind won't work like that. He's a killer.
         He won't have any sense of remorse – only
         resentment at being caught. And you're letting
         him into the house.

TONY   Only once.

MEGAN   Don't you believe it. He'll be back.

TONY   He won't be coming back.

MEGAN   How can you be sure?

TONY   I can make sure . . .

MEGAN   How?

TONY   I can make sure he never leaves . . .

MEGAN   What?

TONY   Todd's offered to kill him for me. Isn't that
         nice of him?

MEGAN   (*stares*) Tony, do you realise what you're
         saying?

TONY   Yes.

MEGAN   He must be mad.

TONY   Yes, but there's method in it – he'll do it for ten
         thousand pounds.

MEGAN   And you're going to pay him?

TONY   I'm not sure.

MEGAN   But you're thinking about it. It seems to me
         he's not the only one who's mad.

TONY   (*shrugs*) I've been mad for a long time. So
            what's new?

MEGAN   This is, Tony. This is real. This isn't talking
            about it. This is doing it.

TONY   You mean it's all been words and empty
            gestures? That's what Todd said.

MEGAN   Tony, you're conspiring to murder. You'll go to
            prison.

TONY   Only if I'm caught. He's never been caught
            before.

MEGAN   (*horrified*) He's done it before?

TONY   He has cuttings. He always gets away with it.

MEGAN   But you won't.

TONY   What if I don't? (*Wildly.*) Think how the
            pictures will increase in value. Remember the
            last time? How my pictures began to sell once
            Alison had been murdered. How I suddenly
            became collectable? Especially when they
            thought I may have done it. Perhaps Todd's
            right. Perhaps Sweeney did me a favour.

MEGAN   Don't torture yourself like that.

TONY   I don't torture myself – she does.

MEGAN   Do you think it'll be easy? That man killed
            your wife. He'll be on his guard.

TONY   He doesn't know why he's here or who I am.

MEGAN   He'll recognise you.

TONY   Not according to Todd. Apparently I look like
          shit.

          (MEGAN *studies him.*)

MEGAN   You may have changed but you can be sure he
          hasn't. He'll still be full of hate for you – and
          dangerous.

TONY   I don't think so. Todd has him on a chain.

MEGAN   And suppose he gets off the chain?

TONY   Megan, you know I've talked about this
          moment for years – what I'd do . . . ?

MEGAN   Yes.

TONY   Well, tonight Todd made me look into myself.
          And do you know what I found? Absolutely
          nothing. He was right. Oh, I found the desire, I
          found the hate but I couldn't find the spirit.

MEGAN   You were being sensible.

TONY   Sensible! Is that what I've come down to?

MEGAN   Why go to prison for that man?

TONY   Why not?

MEGAN   Tony, you have to let her go. She haunts our
          lives. Look in the mirror. You're right, you do
          look like shit. And so do I.

TONY   Megan, I'm in the middle of a dark wood.

MEGAN   We're both in the middle of a dark wood.

TONY   This may be a way out.

MEGAN   No. The way out is to forget her.

TONY   You haven't forgotten her. Why did you tell
             Todd we were having an affair?

MEGAN   (*uneasily*) Did he say that?

TONY   Yes. Why did you?

MEGAN   Because I wanted him to know that your love
             for Alison was less than perfect. That I wasn't
             second best.

TONY   Is that how you feel?

MEGAN   How do you think I feel? I wanted to tell him
             before you showed him the pictures of her from
             your wallet – and told him the clever things she
             said – how she could wear clothes and prepare
             superb meals and how she charmed everyone
             she met.

TONY   Do I do that?

MEGAN   All the time. Oh, and then there'd be her faith
             in your work – how she supported you with her
             money until you began to sell your paintings.

TONY   It's all true.

MEGAN   I know. I'd have supported you, Tony.

TONY   I know you would.

MEGAN   I didn't have the chance.

TONY   I know. I can't forget her, Megan.

MEGAN   (*savagely*) Then kill him.

TONY   What?

MEGAN   Kill him. If that's what it takes to be free of her
          – kill him.

TONY   You don't mean that.

MEGAN   I do. We'll be free of both of them. Two birds
          with one stone. Do it.

TONY   Have you thought of the risk?

MEGAN   Yes, have you?

TONY   I'll be risking my life – everything.

MEGAN   Isn't that what you've always wanted – to risk
          your life for Alison?

TONY   Yes – when it was too late.

MEGAN   How many times have you faced the man with
          the knife, Tony? How many times have you
          saved her? How many times have you stood in
          his way and taken the blows yourself? And died
          for her?

TONY   Every night – in my dreams.

MEGAN   Do you think I didn't know? Well, now's your
          chance.

TONY   Are you sure?

MEGAN   It's put up or shut up, Tony.

TONY   I know.

MEGAN   You don't want to look into yourself again and
          find nothing, do you?

TONY   No.

MEGAN   Then do it. Because he won't let you go. He'll
              be back with all his old complaints of injustice
              and persecution.

TONY   He's confessed his guilt.

MEGAN   He did that to get out, Tony. He did that to get
              out and get at you. But not if you get at him
              first. Draw those curtains.

TONY   Why?

MEGAN   Do you want him to recognise the park? Don't
              they say a murderer always returns to the scene
              of his crime?

TONY   One park looks very much like another – and
              it's growing dark. And he's been drinking.

MEGAN   Don't take any chances. If you are going to do
              it – do it quickly.

TONY   Megan, are you the same person who said I
              should send for the police?

MEGAN   It's too late for the police. I think it always
              was. It's either him or us. I'll walk the dog. I
              won't hurry back. The cheque book's in the top
              drawer of the desk.

TONY   Why are you doing this, Meg?

MEGAN   Because I want you back. And ten thousand
              pounds seems a small price to pay.

TONY   And a man's life?

MEGAN   A man's life. You've never referred to him in
         that way before. Careful, Tony – you'll grow to
         like him.

TONY   I'll never do that.

         (MEGAN *crosses to the door.*)

MEGAN   (*turns*) Should I leave the side door undone for
         them?

TONY   Yes.

         (*She pauses.*)

MEGAN   Where did I say I'd left the cheque book?

TONY   (*sighs*) In the top drawer.

         (*They exchange a glance.* MEGAN *exits.* TONY
         *crosses to the desk and takes out the cheque
         book. He considers it for a moment and then
         puts it back in the drawer. He takes another
         drink. He crosses to the window and looks
         out. He turns back to the desk and then turns
         abruptly. He returns to the windows and
         begins to draw the curtains.* JOE SLATER *enters
         the room followed by* TODD. SLATER *is above
         medium height, rugged, with an air of menace.
         He is in his mid-forties. He crosses silently and
         stands behind* TONY.)

SLATER   Don't do that, guv – let's enjoy the view . . .

         (TONY *turns in surprise.*)

         Pity to shut it out. That's what sells a house
         – the outer aspect. Ask any estate agent. The
         three main selling points – location, location,
         location. Am I right?

TONY   So I've heard.

            (SLATER *looks out.*)

SLATER   And this is a nice location . . . Is that a park?

            (TONY *and* TODD *exchange glances.*)

TONY   Yes.

TODD   (*quickly*) Joe's been rather cooped up of late,
            Tony – he enjoys the feeling of space – can't
            bear to be confined, can you, Joe?

SLATER   Looks familiar . . .

TONY   Would you like a drink?

            (SLATER *turns.*)

SLATER   Why not?

TONY   Only wine I'm afraid.

SLATER   Don't be. I like a glass of wine. I enjoyed a
            very palatable bottle of Chablis over lunch.

TONY   This is red.

SLATER   I like red but it doesn't like me. Know what I
            mean? Gets me fired up. But I'll take it.

            (*He takes the drink. He sips it.*)

            Nice bouquet – no after taste. I'd say a rich
            Burgundy.

            (*He then drains the glass.*)

TONY   You're right.

TODD   You know you're wine, Joe.

        (TODD *refills the glass.*)

SLATER I'm making a study of it.

        (*He sits back and drinks.*)

        How much is a house like this worth, Tony?

TONY   I don't know. I've never had it valued.

SLATER You could be very pleasantly surprised. Money
        in the bank, Tony. There's a lot of equity locked
        up in this house. A bloke with a house like this
        doesn't need to owe money – unless it's heavily
        mortgaged?

TONY   There's no mortgage.

SLATER Then I don't see the problem. Of course a lot of
        people have houses like this and there's nothing
        in the fridge. Know what I mean? You could
        down-size of course. There's just you and your
        wife?

TONY   Yes.

SLATER You must rattle about a bit in a place like this.

TONY   I suppose so.

SLATER Take a bit of hoovering, a place like this. Who
        does it?

TONY   We have people come in.

SLATER What people?

TONY   They call themselves the Merry Maids.

SLATER   (*laughs*) Did you hear that, Toddie? The Merry
              Maids. Jesus! They'd be expensive.

TONY   I don't know. My wife deals with that.

SLATER   She the one who just left?

TONY   Yes.

SLATER   She gave me a look, didn't she, Toddie?

TODD   I didn't see the look, Joe.

SLATER   (*frowns*) There was a look. When I patted the
              dog. As if I wasn't good enough to pat the dog.

TODD   Surely not, Joe.

SLATER   There was a look. Snooty. It's only a bloody
              dog . . .

              (*He rises and looks out of the window again.*
              TONY *continues to watch him.*)

              I suppose you have a gardener?

TONY   Yes.

SLATER   I thought it looked well established. And the
              lawns – I always go by the edges – very well
              manicured.

              (*He turns and catches* TONY'S *stare.*)

              You'll know me next time.

TONY   I feel I know you now . . .

TODD   (*hastily*) Joe enjoys a garden, don't you, Joe?
            One thing you missed. Let me freshen that
            drink.

            (*Refills* SLATER'S *glass.*)

SLATER   You know what gets me? Some people have so
            much and others have nothing. He has all this
            – I haven't even got a window box. Of course
            he could be living above his means. Once he's
            paid the Merry Maids, and the gardener, and
            the rates, holidays abroad skiing, meals in flash
            restaurants – I don't suppose there'd be much
            left over for you, Toddie.

TODD   Oh, I think there would be. You're not living
            above your means, are you, Tony?

TONY   No.

SLATER   Then I can't see the problem. (*Pause.*) What do
            you do?

TODD   Tony's in business.

SLATER   Show me a business man who's got to the top
            and I'll show you a man who's cut a few throats
            on the way up.

TODD   I'm sure Tony hasn't done that. Have you,
            Tony?

TONY   No.

            (*He looks hard at* SLATER.)

            Have you?

SLATER   (*smiles*) That's for me to know – and you to
            find out.

TONY   And what do you do?

SLATER   At the moment I'm a debt collector. (*Frowns.*)
            Take a photograph it'll last longer.

TONY   I'm sorry. For a moment I thought I knew you.

SLATER   Did you? Well, as I said, you'll know me next
            time.

            (TONY *moves closer.*)

TONY   And would you know me next time?

            (SLATER *studies him.*)

SLATER   I doubt it. I put things like this out of my mind.
            You have to move on. You have to or you
            couldn't function. Know what I mean?

TONY   I know what you mean.

SLATER   Did Toddie tell you.

TONY   What?

SLATER   That I'd been inside?

TONY   He did mention it.

SLATER   Did he say why I'd been inside?

TONY   (*pause*) Not in so many words.

SLATER   Can't you guess?

TONY   Something serious?

SLATER	(*laughs*) Well, it wasn't for defacing library books. It was a serious act of violence. It was the big one, Tony. Category A.
TONY	Murder?
SLATER	Does that worry you?
TONY	No.
SLATER	It worries most people. It sets you apart, you see.
TONY	Does it worry you?
SLATER	No. What's the point in worrying? You die if you worry – you die if you don't.
TONY	That's true.
	(SLATER *rises and prowls around the room. He picks up china figure.*)
SLATER	Nice figurine – Meissen, if I'm not mistaken. Yes, Meissen.
	(*He drops the figurine on the floor.*)
	Oh dear. Butter fingers.
TODD	Careful, Joe . . . No need for that.
SLATER	I don't think he's taking me seriously, Toddie. Are you going to pay my friend his money?
TONY	I don't know. I may need twenty-four hours.
SLATER	I don't think that would be acceptable. My friend doesn't believe in extended credit. I know it's gone mad while I've been inside.

Credit card debt is soaring and it's not good for the country. We're staring into an abyss, Tony. It's not good for people. What happens when they all have to pay? Chaos. It's not good for people – and it's not good for you. It gives you a false sense of security. And you'll find out how false if you don't pay Toddie his money . . .

(*Silence.*)

TODD You're right, Joe. I don't think he's taking you seriously.

SLATER (*smiles*) You should, Tony. Because I'm not a very nice person. In fact, I'm a mean bastard.

TONY Aren't you frightened of going back inside?

SLATER That wouldn't worry me. If you can't do the time – don't do the crime, Tony. And I've got some very good mates in there. Apart from the confined space it's not too bad. At least you meet a better class of person. Quite frankly what I've seen since I've been out I've been appalled. Young people drinking in the street – f-ing and blinding. And the rest. Sex at sixteen, Tony. Casual partners – sexually transmitted diseases – they're going into that clinic on skate boards. In my day you got a job at sixteen – and, if you were lucky, you had it away at twenty-one. Now it's the other way around. What's the world coming to? And pornographic films – and dirty books. They're rotting the fabric of society. And what's the church doing about it? Nothing. They're in disarray – they can't even make up their mind if there's a God anymore. They're even letting shirt-lifters become bishops. Where is it going to end, Tony?

(*He sits and puts his feet on the desk.*)

Sorry. How I do go on. I almost forgot what I'm here for . . .

TODD   Do you know something, Joe. I don't think Tony's afraid for himself. I think he's more afraid for his wife . . .

SLATER   You think so?

TODD   But then, perhaps he thinks you're not the sort to hurt a woman . . .

SLATER   Don't count on it, Tony. I'm a great believer in equality. And if they want to be treated like men, they shouldn't complain. And I have it on good authority that some of them actually enjoy it. A bit of rough, Tony. They can find it sexually stimulating. Oh, they can look down their noses and act superior but they can be dying for it. Know what I mean?

TONY   I know what you mean.

SLATER   You should try it some time, Tony. You'd be surprised at the response. Now your old lady for example. She's superior, isn't she? The way she looked when I patted her dog. As if I wasn't good enough. And I'm very good with dogs . . . (*Disparagingly*.) Women!

TODD   When you had to go away, Joe. Was that because of a woman?

SLATER   (*pause*) I'm not saying. Could have been.

TODD   Did she look down on you? Did you try to pat her dog?

SLATER   What?

TODD   Did she make you feel worthless?

SLATER   (*bitterly*) I can't stand those middle class cows
            who stand by the till watching you. Watching to
            see if you put anything in your pockets. I know
            what I'd like to do with them . . .

            (TODD *continues to replenish* SLATER'S *glass.*)

TODD   You see – Joe does have this phobia about the
            middle classes, particularly the women. Don't
            you, Joe?

SLATER   I can't stand them. Lady magistrates, lady
            barristers, prison visitors. Always sitting in
            judgement. And they're no better than I am.
            They need pulling down a peg or two . . .

TODD   This woman, Joe . . . Did you pull her down a
            peg or two?

SLATER   (*grins*) If I did – she deserved it . . .

TODD   Well, let's conclude our business before your
            wife gets back. (*Pause.*) I can give you twenty
            four hours in which to pay . . . or I could take a
            cheque – in which case there'd be no need for
            Joe to call again . . .

            (TONY *regards the sprawling figure of* SLATER *in
            silence.*)

            Well, what is it to be?

            (TONY *slides open the drawer.*)

TONY   I'll make out a cheque.

SLATER   That's more like it.

TONY   Ten thousand, wasn't it?

TODD   Yes.

            (SLATER *straightens up and watches* TONY *make
            out the cheque with avid interest.* TODD *passes
            behind* SLATER. *He removes his glasses and
            places them carefully in his top pocket. He
            takes the garrotte from his side pocket.* TONY
            slides the cheque across the desk.)

            See that the cheque's made out correctly, Joe.

            (SLATER *studies the cheque closely.*)

SLATER   It's not made out to anyone . . .

TODD   That comes later. Is the amount correct?

SLATER   Yes. Ten thousand.

TODD   And the signature. Can you read it?

SLATER   Yes. (*Slowly*) Anthony Reed . . .

TODD   Does that mean anything to you?

SLATER   No.

TODD   It should do. You killed his wife.

SLATER   What!

            (TODD *expertly throws the garrotte over*
            SLATER'S *head and pulls tight.* SLATER'S *chair
            tilts backwards and his legs kick out wildly.*
            TONY *gets up slowly from his chair and crosses
            to the window. He looks out ignoring the
            struggle behind him. He draws the curtains
            and dims the lights, crosses and opens door to*

store room. The light fades to black as the two shadowy figures drag SLATER'S *body through open door of store room. Sound of* TODD *laughing.*)

Curtain.

ACT TWO

The study room. An hour later. It's dark outside. All the lamps are lit.

TONY *is sitting at his desk, drinking and staring at the door of the store room. He starts as* MEGAN *enters. She throws her shoulder bag on a chair and takes off her coat.*

MEGAN   Well?

TONY   It's over.

MEGAN   Where?

TONY   He's in there.

          (MEGAN *advances tentatively towards the store room.*)

          It's locked. Todd has the key. He's bringing his car round.

          (*He crosses and looks out of the window.*)

          I was wrong about Todd. I thought he was without emotion. Cold and detached. But no – he has a nice sense of fun. He actually enjoyed it.

MEGAN   And you didn't.

TONY   No!

MEGAN   You said you would. You said it would give you great pleasure.

TONY   That was before. It took so long.

MEGAN   Nothing dies easily.

TONY   I couldn't have done it.

MEGAN   But you'd let someone else do it.

TONY   I know – you don't have to tell me. I'm a killer
               by proxy.

               (*He pours himself another drink.*)

MEGAN   Not too much of that. There are things to do.

TONY   Oh yes. We have to dispose of the body.
               (*Nervous laugh.*) Very uncooperative, the dead.
               They will lie around.

MEGAN   How are you going to do it?

TONY   Todd drives him out to the far side of the
               common. I follow in my car. There's a spinney.
               We torch the car, it's stolen anyway. Then we
               come back. It's as simple as that.

MEGAN   I don't see why Todd has to involve you. Can't
               his friend help?

TONY   What friend? He hasn't a friend. A man like
               that doesn't have any friends.

MEGAN   I mean his henchman. The man who was with
               him when I left the house.

TONY   That was Sweeney.

MEGAN   Sweeney? (*Stares.*) Did you recognise him?

TONY   Yes. Didn't you?

MEGAN   No.

TONY   Well, it's been a long time.

MEGAN   It may have been a long time but that wasn't
              Sweeney.

TONY   He's changed.

MEGAN   But he hasn't changed! He's no older. You're
              remembering him as he was. That's not how
              he'd be now. He'd have aged. What made you
              think he was Sweeney?

TONY   (*uneasily*) It was him – I know it was.

MEGAN   Did he recognise you?

TONY   Not exactly.

MEGAN   What do you mean – not exactly?

TONY   Well, I've changed, haven't I? It was him. He
              practically boasted about it. He as good as
              admitted it.

MEGAN   Did he admit it?

TONY   (*hesitates*) Not exactly.

MEGAN   We're back to not exactly again.

TONY   I can't remember what he said. He practically
              boasted about it. Why should he do that? Stop
              badgering me.

MEGAN   I'm not badgering you. But you've killed the
              wrong man. I thought I should point that out.

              (*They turn as* TODD *enters.*)

TODD   The car's by the back door.

(*He beams at* MEGAN.)

Ah, you're back, Mrs Reed. Did you enjoy your walk?

MEGAN Not really – it was too dark.

TODD Sooner you than me. If I were Tony I'd worry about you. Walking there alone. And the dog's no protection. Too friendly by half.

MEGAN I can look after myself.

TODD What times we live in. Still, we've rid the world of one evil.

MEGAN Have you?

TONY (*alarmed*) Megan says we killed the wrong man!

TODD But he was pointed out to me. I know he didn't call himself Sweeney but –

MEGAN He didn't call himself Sweeney because he wasn't Sweeney.

TODD (*puzzled*) Ah . . . You mean it's a case of mistaken identity?

TONY What!

MEGAN (*pause*) I don't think it was a mistake . . .

TODD Well, it's been a long time. How can you be sure he wasn't Sweeney?

MEGAN Because you are. You're Sweeney.

(*Silence.*)

TONY   (*appalled*) He's Sweeney?

TODD   I wondered how long it would take you to
            guess.

MEGAN   It's been a long time and you've changed but
            there was something familiar about you . . .
            Then the thought struck me when I was out
            walking. Todd . . . and Sweeney . . . Sweeney
            Todd, the demon barber. You've been playing
            games with us, haven't you?

TONY   (*panicking*) This isn't a game, Megan.

TODD   It certainly isn't. It appears you've killed an
            innocent man, Tony.

TONY   I didn't kill him, you did.

TODD   At your command, Tony. I have a cheque for
            ten thousand pounds to prove it.

TONY   But he boasted – he made me think . . .

TODD   I put him up to that. I told him to frighten you.
            Don't take it too badly. When I say innocent,
            well, he's bound to be guilty of something.
            Something he got away with in the past. That's
            true of all of us. Swings and roundabouts, Tony.

TONY   But he didn't kill Alison.

TODD   Neither did I.

MEGAN   How would you know? You were drunk at the
            time. You wouldn't have remembered. You're
            in denial.

            (TODD *looks at her for a long moment.*)

TODD   Megan, would you check to see if the coast is
            clear? It's time to dispose of our friend.

            (MEGAN *exits*.)

TODD   She's right, of course. I was drunk all the time
            in those days.

TONY   But you're not drunk now. You're cold sober.
            Why did you kill him?TODDTo make a point.

TONY   You killed a man to make a point!

TODD   Isn't that the usual reason?

TONY   (*stares*) What do you want with me?

TODD   The truth.

TONY   You've had the truth. You just won't accept it.

TODD   Do you know why you didn't remember me,
            Tony, whilst I remembered you, vividly?
            Because I was the injured party. The injured
            party always remembers – he's the one who
            suffered.

TONY   What about Alison? Didn't she suffer?

TODD   Don't blame me for Alison.

TONY   My God! You're still pleading your case – I've
            just seen you kill a man.

TODD   The point I was making is that mistakes
            can happen. I was found guilty by dead
            reckoning. The compass pointed to me. But
            dead reckoning can be many miles out. I was a
            drunk. I had a record of petty crime. But once,
            would you believe, I was an educated man.

Drink made a fool of me. I hardly drew a sober breath in those days. By the time I'd dried out I was serving a sentence for murder. It was only then that I began to see things clearly. And then I realised it wasn't the law that hounded me. It was you, Tony. You were my persecutor. You never stopped proclaiming my guilt – to the police – to the press – to anyone who'd listen. Events that would have been forgotten were kept alive by you – the grieving husband.

TONY   Don't blame me. I didn't find you guilty. The evidence was overwhelming.

TODD   Only if you started with the premise that I was guilty. Then everything fitted. But my troubles all began when you saw me, from this window, leaving the park, in a hurry, at the time of the murder.

TONY   So I did.

TODD   From this window. You couldn't even identify me from two feet away!

TONY   You've changed.

TODD   You mean I'm sober. That does make a difference. Oh, you'd seen me in the park – everyone had. I was living rough there. But leaving in a hurry? No. I was walking the streets at that time – in my usual alcoholic haze.

TONY   I saw you.

TODD   You could have been mistaken. You were tonight. And I wouldn't have blamed you for a genuine mistake. But it wasn't genuine, was it, Tony?

TONY   What do you mean?

TODD   I'd only been in prison a year when I received
            a considerable shock. I discovered that the
            inconsolable Anthony Reed had married again.
            The inconsolable had found consolation. I
            know the flesh is weak. But marriage? And
            with such indecent haste. That did surprise me.

TONY   Well, it doesn't surprise you now, does it? You
            know we were lovers.

TODD   Yes, but when I came here tonight, I didn't
            sense that; that you were ever lovers. I didn't
            detect the warm, domestic atmosphere that that
            implies. I found a husband who was drinking
            and a wife on the edge of a breakdown. I felt
            I was in the presence of two people who knew
            where the body was buried, if you'll excuse
            the unfortunate metaphor. And I thought of the
            old adage, *God help people who get what they
            desire most.*

TONY   I don't know where this is leading. You've
            confessed. You must have done to get an early
            release.

TODD   You're right. I confessed. I'd have confessed to
            being Jack the Ripper to get out of that stinking
            hole. But prison did one thing for me – it gave
            me time to think. Think of all those unanswered
            questions. The mystery of the dog that didn't
            bark in the night – whose bite was non-existent.
            A dog who had a court order against it for that
            very thing. A dog fiercely loyal to its mistress.
            What happened to the dog, Tony?

TONY   I had it put down.

TODD   So . . . 'It was the dog that died.'

TONY   What?

TODD   (*quotes*) 'But soon a wonder came to light
                that showed the rogues they lied.
                The man recovered from the bite.
                It was the dog that died.' Goldsmith.

TONY   Goldsmith?

TODD   You appear to like verse. I thought it might
                amuse you.

TONY   It doesn't.

TODD   Why did you have the dog put down?

TONY   It failed her.

TODD   Are you sure that was the only reason? After
                all, the dog was the only one who knew what
                happened. Perhaps you couldn't stand his
                reproachful looks.

TONY   We're wasting time. There's a dead man in
                there.

TODD   He's not going anywhere. I've waited years to
                say all this – pay me the courtesy of listening.
                All right, let's forget the dog.

TONY   By all means.

TODD   Let's get to the bracelet.

TONY   Bracelet?

TODD   Another unanswered question. They kept
                asking me about a bracelet. Gold and coral –
                very expensive. Kept asking me what I'd done
                with it. Then they stopped asking me. It had

been found. I became excited. I thought the murderer may have kept it. But then they told me it had turned up here. In fact, I noticed your wife wearing it tonight.

TONY   I found it in Alison's jewel case. She wasn't wearing it that night.

TODD   But I understood she always wore it.

TONY   Not that night. The catch had become faulty. She was going to have it repaired.

TODD   You see, there's a simple explanation for everything. But a more devious mind may have thought that the murderer may have considered it too valuable to leave behind . . .

TONY   Have you finished?

TODD   You must allow me my day in court.

TONY   You've had your day in court.

TODD   Until I was arrested do you know who the prime suspect would have been?

TONY   No.

TODD   Who is usually the prime suspect in these cases?

TONY   I don't know.

TODD   Why, the husband, Tony. You.

TONY   Really.

TODD   On the day I was charged I heard one of the officers make a remark I didn't understand.

He didn't seem to be sharing the general lust
for my blood. He said he thought it was a gas
meter job. Know what that means, Tony?

TONY   No.

TODD   Neither did I at the time. I found out in
prison. Apparently in the old days when a gas
meter was broken into the culprit was usually
someone in the house – a member of the family.
An inside job. I think Alison's death was a gas
meter job. I wouldn't have suspected it but
that one act of greed over the bracelet. Oh, the
murderer left everything else for me to find,
the purse with the money – the small pieces of
jewellery but not the bracelet. Too valuable – it
may have disappeared . . .

TONY   Do you know what you're doing? The same
thing you said was done to you. You're
assuming I'm guilty and making everything fit.
I married my mistress. She has the bracelet.
I'm guilty. But I wasn't found guilty – you
were. Megan's right, you're in denial. You
don't know what happened that night. You were
sodden with drink, and you're perfectly capable
of killing. I saw that tonight. TODD   But who
pronounced sentence? You did. And do you
know why you pronounced sentence? Because
you thought you were killing Sweeney. It
wasn't revenge. He was the only one who knew
the truth. He had to be silenced – just like the
dog. He was the only one who knew he didn't
kill Alison. Which means someone else did.
(*Pause.*) It haunts you, doesn't it, Tony?

TONY   Not in the least.

TODD   It haunts you in your pictures. I got a lot of
comfort from those pictures. The bleakness
of the backgrounds – the sense of foreboding.

They're the product of a troubled mind. You
didn't really get away with it, did you, Tony?
It is a figure in the shadows, isn't it? Is it you,
Tony?

TONY   If my work has been affected by what happened
        – is that surprising?

TODD   No, you're too good an artist to lie in
        your work. To me it's as good as a written
        confession. You may lie – but your pictures
        can't. There was only one reason why you
        weren't standing in the dock instead of me.

TONY   I had an alibi.

TODD   Suppose I'd had an alibi, Tony? Wouldn't that
        have put the cat amongst the pigeons?

TONY   But you didn't.

TODD   No, I didn't have someone like Megan to speak
        up for me. I'm afraid I've never enjoyed the
        generosity of women.

TONY   Generosity? What has generosity to do with it?

TODD   I had no woman to lie for me.

TONY   You had her purse – you had her jewellery –
        there were blood stains on your clothes.

TODD   The blood stains came from the purse – the
        purse and the jewellery I found by the footpath.
        Where any drifter could have found them
        – where he was meant to find them. How
        fortunate for you, Tony that I wasn't an honest
        man. But then there aren't many about, are
        there? It was a gamble worth taking. But if I'd
        been honest and handed them in you'd have

been in the frame, Tony. Even with an alibi.
And I seem to remember that was slightly
flawed. There was a neighbour who thought he
saw Megan leaving the house earlier . . .

TONY   She was mistaken. She was unreliable. She had
poor eyesight.

TODD   You're right. She made a poor witness –
easily shaken in her testimony. Still, it set me
thinking. As I said you have a lot of time to
think when you're in the slammer. It was then
that I had a little wager with myself. That you
may have said to Megan, 'It's not important
but wouldn't it be a good idea if you said you
were with me at the time of the murder? I
mean, I was here but I can't prove it. It would
save a lot of unnecessary questions. It would
keep things simple – in fact it would help the
investigation – they wouldn't be wasting their
time with me. After all, you know I didn't do
it.' (*Pause.*) Something like that. (*Laughs.*)
Don't look so worried, Tony. It's only a theory.
Pure speculation – it's all circumstantial. Not
enough to send you to prison.

TONY   I'm not worried.

TODD   Then why did you have a man killed tonight?
A man who was just learning about wine – who
may have graduated to good food, and become
a decent member of the middle classes.

TONY   I thought he was the man who killed my wife.

TODD   Now you think I'm the man who killed your
wife. Perhaps you want to kill me?

TONY   No. There's been enough of that.

TODD   Then you have changed. (*He moves closer.*)
            And I wouldn't have recognised you tonight.
            You didn't really get away with it, did you,
            Tony? Is that why you keep painting Alison's
            face? Do you see it all the time?

TONY   Yes!

TODD   You can't live with your guilt, can you, Tony?

TONY   No! (*Shouts.*) I killed her!

TODD   At last.

TONY   I killed her but not in the way you mean. I
            killed her by letting her go out that night,
            alone. I knew there had been muggings, I knew
            there were drifters in the park. I knew there
            were dangers. My crime was simply not caring.

TODD   (*sadly*) Tony, you keep disappointing me.
            That's not a confession.

TONY   That's all you're going to get.

TODD   (*studies him*) When did you start caring, Tony?

TONY   What?

TODD   Caring about Alison?

TONY   Afterwards . . .

TODD   Well, it wasn't when she was late back. That
            was something that always troubled me. You
            didn't go and look for her. You rang the police.
            Why was that?

TONY   It was dark. It's a big park . . .

TODD   You knew the path she took – it never varied.
                Do you know what I think? You didn't go
                and look for her because you knew what you
                were going to find. And you didn't want to be
                discovered at the scene of the crime.

TONY   No!

TODD   You'd have been the prime suspect then, Tony.
                Especially when they discovered you had
                a mistress. But you knew that, didn't you?
                Wasn't it lucky that I came along?

                (MEGAN *enters*.)

MEGAN   There's no one about.

TODD   Then should we get to it?

                Damn! I forgot the shroud. We don't want Joe
                coming unwrapped. Think what the neighbours
                would say. I won't be a moment.

                (*He pauses by the door and smiles.*)

                That's a lovely bracelet, Megan.

                (*He exits.* TONY *and* MEGAN *stare at each other
                in silence for a moment.*)

TONY   I'll need another bottle.

MEGAN   You've had enough.

TONY   Not nearly enough. Why did you have to tell
                him that we were having an affair?

MEGAN   I've already told you. Why?

TONY   He's guessed.

MEGAN   Guessed?

TONY   About the alibi.

MEGAN   He's snatching at straws.

TONY   And you're giving them to him.

MEGAN   He can't prove anything.

TONY   He doesn't need to. He's made up his mind.
           Why did you have to wear that bracelet?

MEGAN   Why not? It's mine. You gave it to me. Don't
           you remember? Shortly after I perjured myself
           for you. And if that woman hadn't been old and
           confused I may have gone to prison.

TONY   I gave you my reasons and you agreed. I
           couldn't prove I was here. They'd have found
           out about us –

MEGAN   Why? Alison didn't. (*Pause.*) Or did she?

TONY   What made you ask that?

MEGAN   I just wondered.

TONY   No, she didn't. Alison had a sweet and trusting
           nature.

MEGAN   Meaning I haven't. Well, neither have you,
           Tony. Isn't that why you married me? Because
           you didn't trust me?

TONY   What do you mean?

MEGAN   Well, the proposal was a surprise. I though
           perhaps you may have married me in the
           mistaken belief that a wife can't give evidence

against her husband. You got that wrong. She
can't be forced to give evidence against her
husband – but she can volunteer it.

TONY   Are you threatening me?

MEGAN   I wouldn't dare. Look what happened to Alison.

(*He raises his hand savagely as if to strike her.
She flinches from him giving the impression
that this has happened before. He hesitates.*)

TONY   I'm sorry.

MEGAN   Why? It's not as if it's the first time. You can
be quite violent can't you, Tony? I wouldn't
have married you if I'd known that. After all,
they say we're more in danger from our loved
ones than from strangers. I believe statistics
prove it. Often when we think we're locking
danger out – we're locking danger in . . .

TONY   I didn't marry you to silence you.

MEGAN   I'll have to take your word for that.

TONY   (*pause*) Do you think I'm a danger?

MEGAN   Do you know something? I always thought you
could have done it.

TONY   What!

MEGAN   So that we could be together. First there was
the alibi – followed by the excessive grief –
followed by the discovery of the bracelet. Then
there was the dog. He wouldn't have bitten you,
would he? He trusted you – just as Alison did.
Then there was the way you began to rail about
Sweeney. You protested too much. As if you

were afraid the finger may be pointed at you.
You reminded me of those people who make
those tear stained appeals for the return of their
loved ones knowing all the time where they're
buried.

TONY   For God's sake, Megan. I protested too much
              because I felt guilty. But feeling guilty isn't the
              same as being guilty. Don't you believe me?

MEGAN   I want to believe you. But wanting to believe
              you isn't the same as believing you, is it? I
              want to believe you because I still love you
              – although you make it harder every year.
              Because I loved you I perjured myself for you.
              I didn't care if I sent an innocent man to prison
              as long as I could have you.

TONY   Innocent! I saw him kill a man tonight. If he
              could kill once he could kill twice. He killed
              Alison – he killed Slater.

MEGAN   And he could kill again. I suppose it gets easier
              – like adultery.

TONY   (*sharply*) Why did you say that?

MEGAN   Well, I wasn't the first, was I, Tony – and I
              don't suppose I'll be the last.

TONY   You see what he's doing to us?

MEGAN   I told you he'd find us one day.

TONY   I'll never be free of him.

MEGAN   Not while he has that cheque.

TONY   What do you mean?

MEGAN   That's the only thing that ties you in with him.

TONY   Well, he's not going to give it back.

MEGAN   Not willingly. But we could take it.

TONY   How? When?

MEGAN   When he's dead.

TONY   What?

MEGAN   There's room in that car for more than one.

TONY   Do you realise what you're saying?

MEGAN   It's our only way out.

TONY   You're not being rational.

MEGAN   Is he being rational? We're in his crazy world now – with his crazy rules – and we're dancing to them.

TONY   We couldn't do it.

MEGAN   We could together.

TONY   We'll be caught. It takes careful planning – attention to detail. Sweeney said that.

MEGAN   Is that how he planned this evening?

TONY   Yes.

MEGAN   Then his plan can serve for both of them.

TONY   But he's strong. We could never do it.

MEGAN   You could do it. You're strong. You could do it.

TONY   Because you still think I killed Alison?

MEGAN   No, because he won't be expecting it. He
             doesn't see you as a threat. He holds you in
             contempt whilst he plays God. Well, let God
             die.

             (*She pours him the last of the wine.*)

             Finish this. I'll get you another bottle.

TONY   He scares the shit out of me, Megan.

MEGAN   Not for much longer. You can do it. They say
             that we become the thing we fear most. Well,
             become Sweeney, Tony. Become a killer.

TONY   I don't think I can.

MEGAN   It has to be done.

             (TODD *enters with a cloth draped over his arm.*)

TODD   What has to be done, Megan?

TONY   (*quickly*) Moving the body. I'm not looking
             forward to it.

TODD   Soon be over, Tony. The coast is clear, so we
             may as well get on with it . . .

             (*He unlocks the door and peers in.*)

             Now to get rid of the rubbish. Ah. What's this?

             (*He enters and returns with* TONY's *painting.*)

Your painting. He was sprawled all over it.
Obviously no respect for art. You shouldn't
have hidden it away, Tony. I think it's one
of your best. And so typical. (*He studies the
picture.*) The same cheerful foreground – the
same forbidding shadows in the background.
And there is a figure in the shadows – I can
see it now quite clearly. It seems to be moving
forward.

TONY   You're not here to discuss my work.

TODD   It's a park scene, isn't it? And isn't that a lady
          with a dog?

          (TONY *snatches the canvas from him.*)

TONY   It isn't finished.

          (*He stands the canvas facing the wall.*)

TODD   I'm sorry. I didn't mean to ruffle the artistic
          temperament. (*Pause.*) Well, down to business.
          Would you prefer the head or the feet?

TONY   What?

TODD   The feet, I think. After you, Tony . . .

          (TONY *hesitates at the threshold.* TODD *shoves
          him into the store room, closes the door and
          locks it. There is a muffled cry of protest from*
          TONY.)

MEGAN   (*shocked*) What are you doing?

TODD   I'm having fun.

MEGAN   You'll drive him mad.

(*Cries and banging from* TONY.)

TODD   Tony, please – not so much noise. You'll wake
            the dead.

TONY   (*off*) Why are you doing this?

TODD   You wanted red meat, Tony. Well, now you're
            in the abattoir. How does it feel? You wanted
            to see a man die in his shoes – you've got what
            you desired most. Isn't it what you expected?

TONY   (*sobbing*) Please – let me out.

TODD   Is it a bit crowded in there? I was in a cell not
            much bigger than that for years. I was a caged
            beast, Tony. I went a little mad.

            (MEGAN *pulls* TODD *away from the door.*)

MEGAN   You can't do this to him.

TODD   (*angrily*) Can't? Can't? I'm doing it. What's the
            matter, Tony? Don't you like sharing? Don't
            you care for your companion? He doesn't say
            much does he? Would you say rather formal – a
            little on the stiff side? Did he move, Tony? No,
            surely not. What about the stare, Tony? Does it
            worry you? Does he seem to be watching you?
            I could switch the light out.

            (*He flicks the switch on the outside of the door.
            A cry of protest from* TONY.)

            Now at least you can't see him. But is he
            moving, Tony? I think he may be.

            (*Loud banging on the door.*)

(*sharply*) Be quiet, Tony – or I'll leave you there all night. You'll be white haired in the morning. Do you want that? All I want is the truth about what happened the night Alison died . . .

(*He picks up the canvas and studies it.*)

I'm looking at the picture, Tony. I can definitely see a figure in the shadows. And it certainly looks familiar. Is it you, Tony? I think it might be. Tell me the truth. Is it?

TONY   (*sobbing*) Yes! I killed her. Let me out for God's sake!

TODD   Did you hear that, Megan? The truth at last.

MEGAN   He'd say anything to get out of there.

TODD   You're right. You won't change your mind when you get out of there, will you, Tony. You won't retract?

TONY   No!

TODD   Then tell me what really happened that night. Think hard. Think back. Deep in your subconscious is the truth – and you buried it, Tony.

TONY   I'll tell you everything, only let me out.

TODD   Tell me first, Tony . . .

            (MEGAN *picks up her shoulder bag and crosses to* TODD.)

MEGAN   Let him out.

TODD   Not yet.

                (MEGAN *takes a knife from her bag.*)

MEGAN   Let him out.

                (TODD *stares and takes a step back.*)

TODD   So that's why you aren't afraid to walk the
                park.

                (*He unlocks the door.* TONY *emerges clutching
                his chest. He backs fearfully from the door.*)

TONY   I heard it. It made a noise.

TODD   The dead often do, Tony. They're like empty
                houses when the living have departed – they
                groan and creak.

TONY   And I thought it moved.

TODD   Moved? Then we'd better lock the door again.
                We don't want old Joe chasing you out of the
                house.

                (*He locks the door again.* TONY *sees the knife
                in* MEGAN'S *hand for the first time.*)

TONY   What are you doing with that?

TODD   Surprised, Tony? Well, you aren't the first
                husband to be surprised by the contents of his
                wife's handbag.

MEGAN   It's for protection.

TODD   Protection? Against me?

MEGAN   Yes.

TODD   I thought it might be for quite another reason.

TONY   What's that?

TODD   I thought you might be planning to kill me.

(MEGAN *and* TONY *share a glance.*)

MEGAN   Don't be ridiculous . . .

(*She puts the knife down on the desk.*)

TONY   What on earth made you think that?

TODD   I thought it might be the next step. Kill me and get the cheque back. Didn't you even discuss it? Have you never thought about it? I would have done.

TONY   But you're a killer.

TODD   So are you. You've just told me so.

TONY   How would I kill you. I don't have the knife.

TODD   But Megan does. Megan has a knife. And 'How oft the means to do ill deeds . . . makes ill deeds done . . .' (*Smiles.*) Shakespeare.

TONY   She has the knife because she's afraid.

TODD   Afraid? A woman who walks the park at night? Married to a man who's confessed to murder. I'm the one who should be afraid. Do you wish me dead? Which, I would hastily point out, is not the same as doing it.

TONY   Yes. My God, we do.

TODD   And did you wish Alison dead? The two of
            you? Which, again, is not the same as doing it.

TONY   No.

TODD   Never? Never even discussed it? 'If anything
            happened to Alison?'

TONY   We may have discussed it.

TODD   'If anything happened to Alison we could be
            together always . . .' The great euphemism.
            What was going to happen? Was she going to
            be abducted by aliens? No, what you mean by
            'if anything happened' – what we all mean by
            'if anything happened' is death. Did you wish
            her dead?

TONY   No!

MEGAN   I did.

TONY   What?

MEGAN   Every time she went on a journey – caught a
            train or a plane – drove her car too fast – went
            into that park at night . . . I hoped something
            would happen.

TODD   Something? Another euphemism? Don't you
            mean death?

MEGAN   Yes! Death!

TONY   Would you leave Megan out of this?

TODD   By all means.

TONY   You heard me confess.

Todd   Yes. But you were locked in a cupboard with a
        dead man. And as Megan observed you'd have
        said anything, even your prayers, to get out of
        there.

Tony   Then you don't believe me?

Todd   I'm not sure. Sad, isn't it? I've spent most of
        the evening trying to get you to confess and
        now I'm not sure I believe you. You see there's
        a flaw. There's a flaw in my case against you.
        Didn't you spot it tonight?

Tony   No.

Todd   You'd never have made a detective. There was
        a flaw in my argument. When I was in full cry
        after you. I saw this flaw. And it pulled me up
        short.

Tony   What are you talking about?

Todd   When I was pressing you on the question of
        why you didn't dare to go near the body.

Tony   I don't understand.

Todd   The footprints, Tony – the footprints. You could
        have washed off the blood but you couldn't
        remove the footprints.

Tony   What footprints?

Todd   (sighs) You're forcing me to act for the
        defence, Tony. It had rained for days. The
        ground was soft. I was living rough in the park.
        My footprints were everywhere. That's why
        they were near the body. But where were yours,
        Tony? Alison fell where she was stabbed.
        And she died where she fell. There had to be

footprints. And there were – mine and hers. But where were yours? You couldn't have removed them. You couldn't even see them in the dark. No, you'd have to make sure you found her first. That way your footprints, if there were any, would have been explained. But you didn't find her first, did you, Tony? You didn't even go and look for her. You called the police. So, what I thought was an act of guilt was, in fact, the act of an innocent man. Annoying, isn't it?

MEGAN   And since yours were the only footprints – doesn't that point to your guilt?

TODD   Who knows? By the time the police had finished it was a quagmire. But I didn't say that mine were the only footprints.

TONY   But you did.

TODD   I said there were mine and Alison's.

TONY   The same thing.

TODD   Not the same thing. There were the heavy footprints of a man, mine – and the light footprints of a woman . . .

TONY   Alison's.

TODD   What no one thought about – neither the defence, or the prosecution, and certainly not me, was there could have been two women. And two sets of footprints.

TONY   What?

MEGAN   I think he means me.

TODD   We'll never know now, Megan. The footprints
            have long since been washed away. Certainly
            they were never checked.

TONY   You suspect Megan?

TODD   Well, one thing's certain, Alison didn't kill
            herself.

TONY   No – you killed her.

TODD   So we're back to me again.

TONY   You've made a very good case against yourself.

TODD   And I thought I was making a good case against
            Megan.

TONY   It may interest you to know that Megan has
            always thought I killed Alison. Does that
            surprise you?

TODD   Not really.

TONY   She always suspected me. It ate away at her. It
            was because of that that she couldn't make love
            to me.

TODD   She thought that you'd killed Alison?

TONY   Yes. And tonight she virtually accused me.

TODD   Tonight? You don't think that was because she
            felt cornered – she felt the net closing.

TONY   No.

TODD   When you told her you were having Sweeney
            killed – did she object?

TONY   At first.

TODD   At first. But not for long. He was her only
            threat – get rid of him and the rest was silence.
            Most wives would have said – don't be a fool
            – go to the police. But not Megan. And who
            suggested killing me tonight? I know it was
            talked about. Was that Megan?

            (*Silence.*)

            I thought so. And you think because she
            accused you that makes her innocent? Don't be
            naïve, Tony. She was getting her accusation in
            first.

MEGAN   Why are you listening to him? You don't
            believe him?

TONY   No.

TODD   No – but then he doesn't quite believe you,
            Megan. He never has. What games married
            couples play . . .

MEGAN   What are you trying to say?

TODD   You couldn't make love to him because he
            couldn't make love to you! You shouldn't
            have blamed yourself, Megan. You can't love
            someone who doesn't respond.

MEGAN   That was the drink.

TODD   No, it went deeper than that. So deep that
            even Tony didn't know why. But it showed
            in his paintings. It showed that he had . . .
            misgivings. Why do you think he persecuted
            me with such vigour – because the alternative
            was too dreadful to contemplate.

MEGAN   What misgivings? What alternative?

TODD   It's in the painting, Megan. That's why he
             didn't want to show it to you. The figure in the
             shadows . . .

             (*He picks up the canvas and holds it in front of
             him. He advances towards her.*)

             You can see it quite clearly now – because
             it's getting closer. And you can see that it's a
             woman. And what's that in her hand? Could it
             be a knife?

             (MEGAN *peers closely at the painting. She looks
             up at* TODD'S *triumphant smile.*)

             It's you, isn't it, Megan?

             (MEGAN *is breathing heavily. She snatches
             the knife from the desk and thrusts it through
             the canvas and into* TODD'S *body.* TODD *gasps
             and staggers back, dropping the canvas. He
             clutches his side and sinks into a chair. He
             looks at the blood on his hand.*)

TONY   Megan!

MEGAN   I told him. I tried to warn him. Interfere in
             people's lives and things happen . . .

             (*She pulls back the blade as if to strike again.*
             TONY *stands in the way. She shrugs and moves
             away.*)

             It's of no consequence. He'll die soon enough.

             (TODD *speaks with an effort.*)

TODD   I'm afraid she's right, Tony. After all, she's
               something of an expert . . .

               (*His head begins to fall forward.*)

TONY   He needs a doctor.

               (TONY *moves to the telephone.* MEGAN *checks
               him.*)

MEGAN   Why? Isn't this what you wanted? To kill
               Sweeney? You've talked about it often enough.
               Well, now it's done.

TONY   That was when I thought he'd killed Alison.

MEGAN   And now you don't?

TONY   (*pause*) I was never sure.

MEGAN   You've never been sure about anything, have
               you, Tony? You always thought it might be me.
               It's true, isn't it. (*She picks up picture.*) I am
               the one in the picture, aren't I, Tony?

TONY   Yes.

MEGAN   When? When did you think it might be me?

TONY   When you suggested the alibi.

MEGAN   As long ago as that?

TONY   You weren't with me when Alison died. You
               must have been on your way home. When you
               said you'd tell the police I was with you I was
               grateful. Later, it occurred to me that this gave
               you an alibi too.

MEGAN   You never said a word.

TONY   I didn't want to believe it. I shut it out.

MEGAN Not in your pictures, Tony.

     (She throws down the picture. TONY *looked anxiously at the crumpled figure of* TODD *and crosses to the phone.)*

     No. It's too late for that.

     (She takes the phone from him and replaces it.)

     Should we tidy things up?

     *(*TONY *watches horrified as* MEGAN *searches* TODD'S *pockets. She produces the cheque and the key.)*

     We'll have to get rid of them both.

TONY   What!

     (She hands him the key.)

MEGAN You're going to get your hands dirty at last, Tony. *(She nods towards the store room)*. We have to get him out of there – and I can't lift him on my own.

     *(*MEGAN *hands him the key and pushes him towards the door. She crosses, dims lights and checks the window.* TONY *hesitates and unlocks the door. He is about to open the door when he takes his hand from the door knob as if stung. He starts back from the door.)*

MEGAN *(from the window)* What's the matter?

TONY   The handle – I felt it turn!

MEGAN   Don't be ridiculous.

               (*The door bursts open and* TONY *cries out in
               terror as* SLATER'S *shadowy figure emerges from
               the room.*)

TONY   My God!

SLATER   Thought I was dead, didn't you, Tony? Perhaps
               I am – perhaps I'm a ghost come back to
               haunt you. On the other hand perhaps I'm
               indestructible.

               (*He advances.* TONY *falls back.*)

TONY   I saw him kill you!

SLATER   And you think seeing is believing? Not in this
               case, Tony, my old son.

               (*He takes hold of* TONY. MEGAN *snaps on
               lights.*)

MEGAN   (*sharply*) Leave him!

               (SLATER *turns and sees* MEGAN *for the first time.
               He takes in the knife and then the whole scene.*)

SLATER   Hang about, lady. No need for violence.
               (*Observes* TODD.) What's the game, Toddie?

TODD   The game, Joe, is up.

SLATER   I didn't bargain for this.

MEGAN   What did you bargain for, Joe?

SLATER   I met Toddie inside. He said there was money
               in it. He didn't say anything about knives. He
               said I could have the money – all he wanted

was the truth. We were going to scare the shit
out of Tony. I was supposed to come back from
the dead – and he'd spill his guts. Toddie didn't
say anything about knives.

TODD   Now I'm the one spilling his guts, Joe.

            (SLATER *is moving towards the door*.)

MEGAN   There's still money in it Joe. Ten thousand
            pounds. It's yours.

            (*She hands him the cheque*.)

SLATER   (*studies it*) There's blood on it.

MEGAN   They'll still cash it. All you have to do is carry
            him to the car.

            (TONY *checks* TODD'S *pulse*.)

TONY   We can't leave him like this.

MEGAN   (*patiently*) We're not leaving him like this.
            We're taking him to the car.

TONY   And then?

MEGAN   (*hesitates*) We'll see . . .

TONY   Like you saw about Alison?

MEGAN   What?

            (TONY *crosses to the phone*.)

MEGAN   What are you doing?

TONY   Dialling 999.

SLATER   I'm out of here.

              (*He throws down the cheque and exits.* TONY
              picks up the phone. MEGAN *advances with the*
              knife extended.)

MEGAN   Don't be a fool, Tony.

TONY   I've been a fool.

MEGAN   Put the phone down.

              (TONY *slowly lays the phone on the desk. They*
              stand for a moment. MEGAN *turns the knife*
              around and hands it to him. He takes it.)

MEGAN   (*smiles*) Now it's your word against mine,
              Tony.

TONY   (*quietly*) It always was.

              (*She exits.* TONY *hesitates and slowly replaces*
              the phone. Half turns towards the door.)

TODD   (*raises himself with an effort*) It was the dog
              that died, after all, Tony . . .

              (TONY *hesitates again. He picks up the phone.*
              Dials.)

TONY   Hello. Police and ambulance. Park View. Park
              Crescent. Hurry . . .

              (*Curtain. The end.*)